Idaho
The Gem State

Marcia Amidon Lusted

PowerKiDS
press™

New York

Published in 2011 by The Rosen Publishing Group, Inc.
29 East 21st Street, New York, NY 10010

First Edition

Editor: Maggie Murphy
Book Design: Greg Tucker
Layout Design: Kate Laczynski
Photo Researcher: Jessica Gerweck

Photo Credits: Cover Stephen Saks/Getty Images; p. 5 Darlyne A. Murawski/Getty Images; pp. 7, 22 (Sacagawea) MPI/Getty Images; p. 9 Bob Pool/Getty Images; p. 11 Karl Weatherly/Getty Images; pp. 13, 17, 22 (flower) Shutterstock.com; p. 15 © Glenn Oakley/age fotostock; p. 19 © Julian Pottage/age fotostock; p. 22 (tree) Wikimedia Commons; p. 22 (fruit) Jonathan Buckley/Getty Images; p. 22 (bird) © www.istockphoto.com/Frank Leung; p. 22 (Sarah Palin) Chip Somodevilla/Getty Images; p. 22 (Merril Hoge) Paul Jasienski/Getty Images.

Library of Congress Cataloging-in-Publication Data

Lusted, Marcia Amidon.
    Idaho : the Gem State / Marcia Amidon Lusted. — 1st ed.
        p. cm. — (Our amazing states)
    Includes index.
    ISBN 978-1-4488-0661-4 (library binding) — ISBN 978-1-4488-0755-0 (pbk.) — ISBN 978-1-4488-0756-7 (6-pack)
    1. Idaho—Juvenile literature. I. Title.
    F746.3.L87 2011
    979.6—dc22
                                    2009050108

Manufactured in the United States of America

CPSIA Compliance Information: Batch #WS10PK: For Further Information contact Rosen Publishing, New York, New York at 1-800-237-9932

Contents

Welcome to Idaho

There is a state where you can find **precious gems** and metals like gold, silver, and garnet. You can also climb mountains and ski down snowy slopes. **Astronauts** even train for space **missions** here. Where are you? You are in Idaho!

Idaho is located in the Pacific Northwest part of the United States. Oregon and Washington border it to the west. Its eastern border touches Montana. To the north is the country of Canada.

Idaho is known for its beautiful scenery. It has amazing mountains, gleaming lakes, and the famous Shoshone Falls. They are even taller than Niagara Falls. Idaho is a wonderful place for anyone who loves the outdoors.

4

Seeing the Shoshone Falls, shown here, is one of the many reasons people visit Idaho. Springtime is the best time of the year to see the falls.

A Place to Explore

The first people to live in Idaho were Native Americans like the Shoshone and Paiute peoples. The land that makes up present-day Idaho was part of the Louisiana Purchase. The United States bought this land from France in 1803.

President Thomas Jefferson sent Meriwether Lewis and William Clark west in 1804 to **explore** the new land. With the help of their Native American guide, a woman named Sacagawea, they visited Idaho and met people from native tribes.

Later Idaho became part of the Oregon Trail, a wagon trail leading from Missouri to Oregon. **Pioneers** from the East settled there. Soon gold was found, and many more people came to Idaho, hoping to get rich. In 1890, Idaho became the forty-third state.

This painting of the Lewis and Clark expedition shows Sacagewea (standing, second from right) speaking with Chinook Indians in the boat to the left.

A Land of Precious Gems

Idaho has 80 different mountain ranges, including the Rocky Mountains. It also has high **plateaus** and deep valleys, rivers, and lakes. Idaho's Coeur d'Alene Lake is one of those beautiful lakes. The Shoshone Falls, on the Snake River, are 212 feet (65 m) high.

Idaho gets its nickname, the Gem State, from the many different precious gems and metals mined in its mountains. Garnets, opals, and sapphires, as well as gold, silver, and copper, are found in Idaho.

Idaho does not get as cold in the winter as some other mountain states do. Summers can be cool and wet. Idaho's mountains can get as much as 30 feet (9 m) of snow every year!

Here, the snow-covered tops of the Sawtooth Mountains are seen on a snowy winter day near Stanley, Idaho.

Skis, Rafts, and Kayaks

With its many mountains and rivers, Idaho is a great place for outdoor sports. One of the biggest sports there is skiing. People come to ski on the famous dry, powdery snow. Idaho's Sun Valley **Resort** is one of America's oldest ski resorts. Movie stars go there to ski. People who have skied in the Olympic Games go there to practice.

Idaho is also a great place for rafting and kayaking. Visitors can kayak on quiet rivers. For more excitement, they can raft through white-water rapids on the Snake River. Other popular sports in Idaho include mountain biking, hiking, and hang gliding. You can even travel by dog sled or float through the air in a hot-air balloon!

This family is enjoying a hike through Sun Valley, in central Idaho, in the springtime. In the wintertime, people enjoy snow sports at the resort.

Have Some Huckleberries

Idaho is home to many different plants and animals. Evergreen forests cover many parts of the state, especially the mountains. There, ponderosa and lodgepole pines grow, as well as aspen, maple, and mountain ash trees.

Idaho is also known for the delicious huckleberries that grow wild in the mountains. These small, round purple berries are a treat for both humans and bears. The huckleberry is Idaho's state fruit.

Many animals can be found in Idaho, including grizzly bears, bighorn sheep, elk, and gray wolves. Whooping cranes, which are an **endangered species**, can be found in the Grays Lake National Wildlife Refuge. Several kinds of trout swim in Idaho's waters.

The whooping crane, shown here, is one of 200 species of mammals, birds, fish, and amphibians you can find at the Grays Lake National Wildlife Refuge.

Made in Idaho

When many people think of Idaho, they think of potatoes. Idaho grows more potatoes than any other state. Farmers there also grow wheat, peas, beans, and sugar beets. Cattle are raised for meat and dairy goods, and fish hatcheries raise many types of seafood.

Factories in Idaho make many kinds of **electronics**. Lumber is cut from its forests. Other factories process food, such as the potatoes and sugar beets grown in the state. Precious metals and gems can still be found in Idaho's mines.

Many visitors come to Idaho to ski and see beautiful scenery. Because of this, lots of people there have jobs that provide food, places to stay, and fun things to do for these visitors.

Here, Idaho potatoes are loaded onto trucks so that they can be sold at stores and markets throughout the country.

The City of Trees

Idaho's capital is Boise. Because the city has so many trees, people call it the City of Trees. It was originally built to be near the Oregon Trail. The Boise River flows through the middle of the city, with many parks along its banks.

Idaho's state capitol looks like very much like the U.S. Capitol, in Washington, D.C. Across the street is the old Union Pacific Railroad Depot, which was built in 1925. Train service there ended in 1971. Now, the city gives tours of the building and holds special events there.

In Boise, you can visit the Zoo Boise or explore science at the Discovery Center of Idaho. You can also see amazing works of art at the Boise Art Museum.

Idaho's state capitol was built between 1905 and 1920. Most of the sandstone used to build the capitol was taken from Table Rock, near Boise, Idaho.

Volcanoes and Astronauts

Thousands of years ago, ancient **volcanoes** erupted and **lava** spread across part of what is now Idaho. These lava flows hardened, creating a rock called basalt. Cinder cones, spatter cones, and lava tubes are some of the other natural formations left behind by the lava. Today this area is Idaho's Craters of the Moon National Monument and Preserve. Visitors can see these formations and the plants and animals that live there.

Because the area looks like the surface of the Moon, *Apollo 14* astronauts came here in 1969 before their trip to the Moon. They learned about **geology** and how to gather rocks. They used what they learned there to help them identify rock features on the Moon and bring back Moon rocks.

Here, the landscape of Craters of the Moon is seen from the Inferno Cone Viewpoint. The Inferno Cone is one of the preserve's many famous cinder cones.

Something for Everyone

Idaho is a great place to visit. You can spend your time skiing at Sun Valley or rafting on the Snake River. You might also like to learn about pioneer times, the gold rush, or the travels of Lewis and Clark. Feeling warm? You can visit the Crystal Ice Cave and see a frozen waterfall.

There are also Native American festivals and museums where you can learn about the native peoples who first lived in Idaho. Are you in the mood for ghosts? You can travel the Yankee Fork Historic Loop and visit deserted gold mines and ghost towns. No matter what you like to do, Idaho has something for everyone!

Glossary

astronauts (AS-truh-nots) People who are trained to travel in outer space.

electronics (ih-lek-TRAH-niks) Objects that are powered by electricity.

endangered species (in-DAYN-jerd SPEE-sheez) Kinds of animals that will likely die out if people do not keep them safe.

explore (ek-SPLOR) To travel over little-known land.

gems (JEMZ) Precious stones that may be worn as decoration.

geology (jee-AH-luh-jee) The makeup of rocks and minerals on a certain surface.

lava (LAH-vuh) A hot liquid made of melted rock that comes out of a volcano during an eruption.

missions (MIH-shunz) Special jobs or tasks.

pioneers (py-uh-NEERZ) Some of the first people to settle in a new area.

plateaus (pla-TOHZ) Broad, flat, high pieces of land.

precious (PREH-shus) Having a high value or price.

resort (rih-ZORT) A place people go to have fun.

volcanoes (vol-KAY-nohz) Openings in the surface of Earth that sometimes shoot up a hot liquid rock called lava.

Idaho State Symbols

State Tree
Western White
Pine

State Fruit
Huckleberry

State Flag

State Bird
Mountain
Bluebird

State Flower
Syringa

State Seal

Famous People from Idaho

Sacagawea
(c. 1788–1812)
Born Near Present-Day
Lemhi, ID
Native American
Interpreter

Sarah Palin
(1964–)
Born in Sandpoint, ID
Former Alaska Governor

Merril Hoge
(1965–)
Born in Pocatello, ID
Sportscaster

Idaho State Map

Priest Lake

Pend Oreille Lake

Coeur d'Alene

Coeur d'Alene Lake

Dworshak Reservoir

Lewiston

Clearwater Mountains

Bitterroot Range

Salmon River

Salmon

Salmon River Mountains

Sawtooth Mountains

Smoky Mountains

Boise

Idaho Falls

Rocky Mountains

Snake River

Pocatello

Twin Falls

Bear Lake

Legend

○ Major City

★ Capital

〰 River

Idaho State Facts

Population: About 1,293,955

Area: 82,747 square miles (214,314 sq km)

Motto: "Let It Be Perpetual"

Song: "Here We Have Idaho," words by McKinley Helm and Albert J. Tompkins, music by Sallie Hume-Douglas

Index

Web Sites

Due to the changing nature of Internet links, PowerKids Press has developed an online list of Web sites related to the subject of this book. This site is updated regularly. Please use this link to access the list:

www.powerkidslinks.com/amst/id/

24